High Jinks

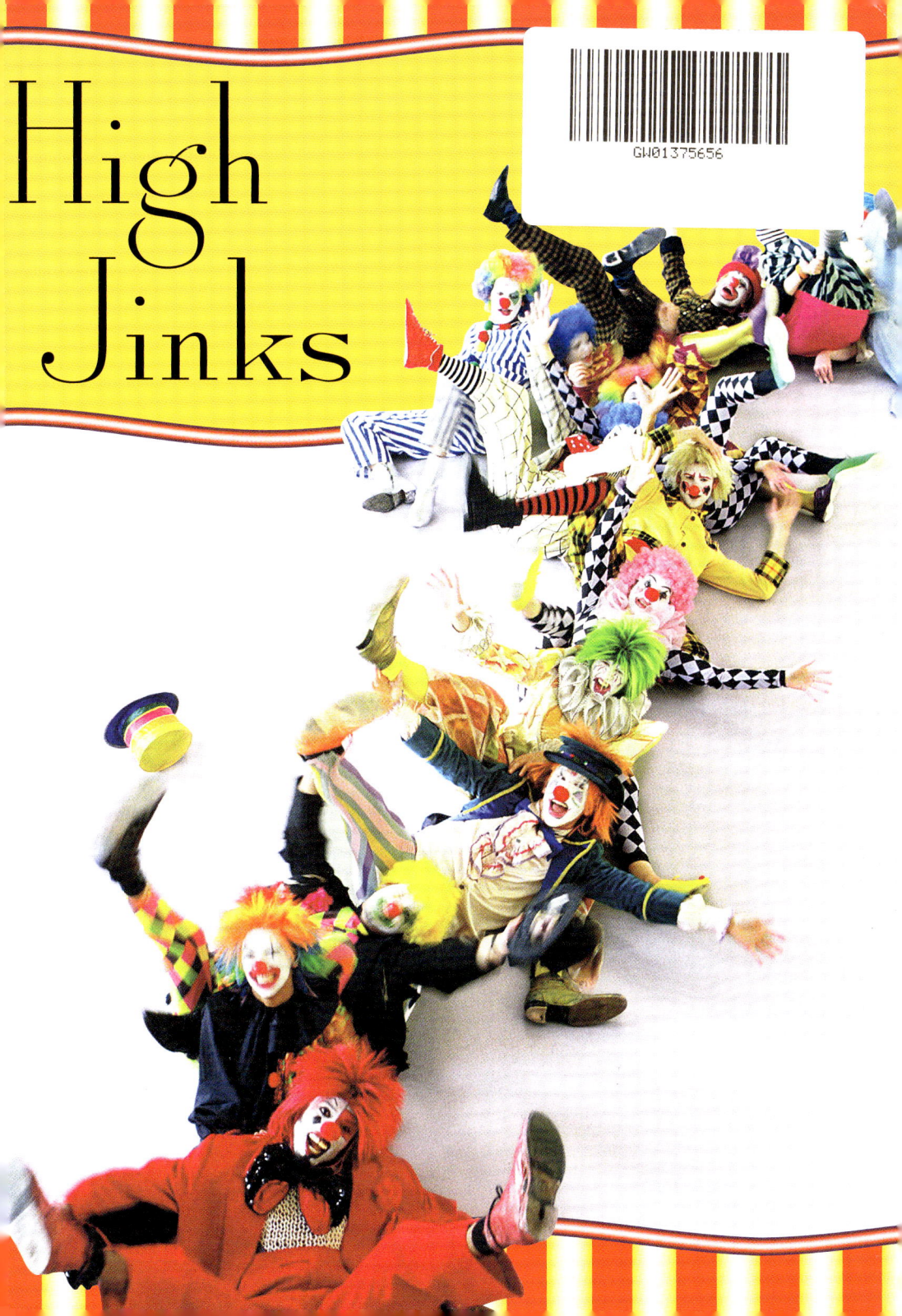

Contents

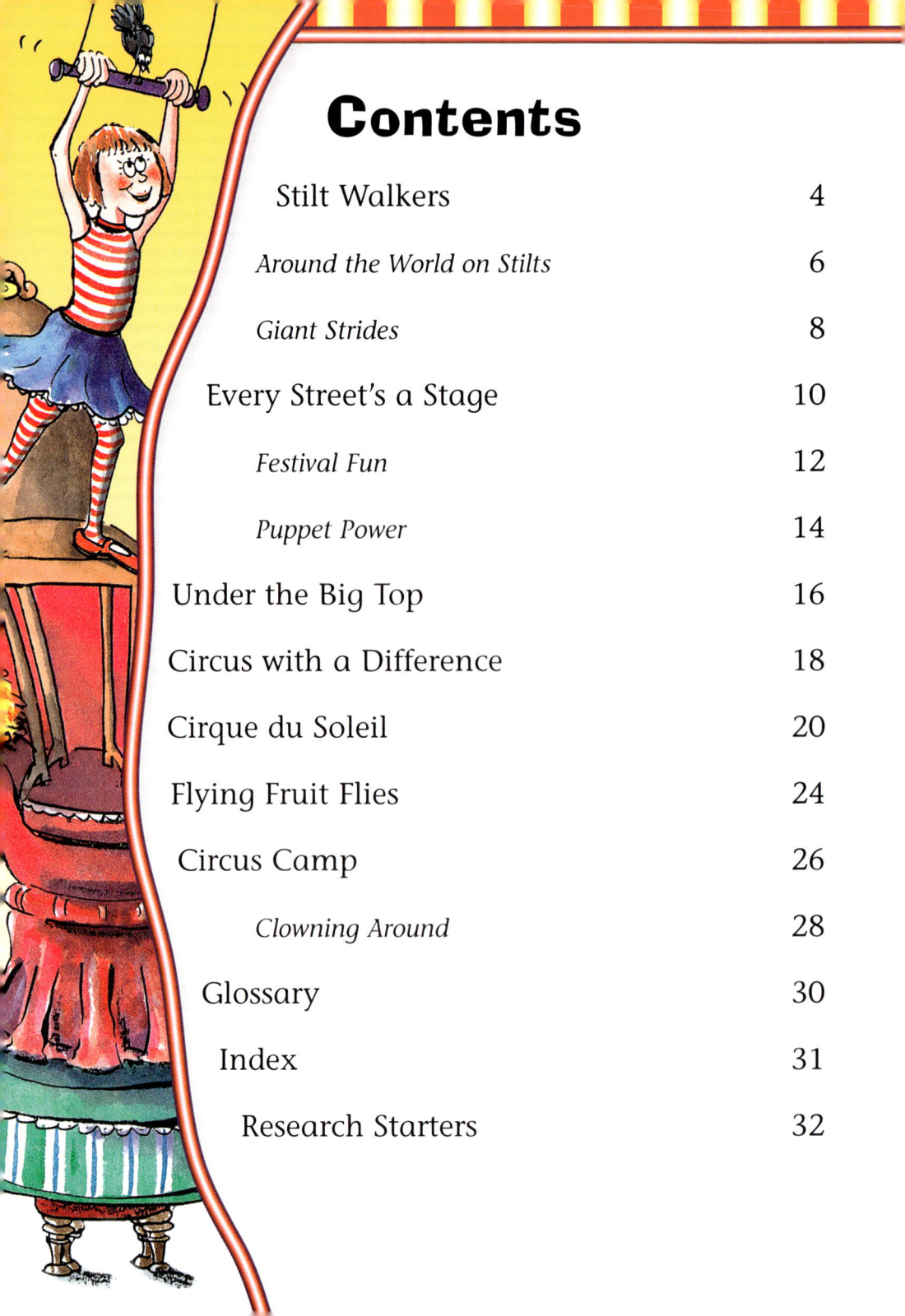

Stilt Walkers	4
Around the World on Stilts	6
Giant Strides	8
Every Street's a Stage	10
Festival Fun	12
Puppet Power	14
Under the Big Top	16
Circus with a Difference	18
Cirque du Soleil	20
Flying Fruit Flies	24
Circus Camp	26
Clowning Around	28
Glossary	30
Index	31
Research Starters	32

Features

IN FOCUS

Read an interview with a professional stilt walker and learn how he trained in **Tall Talk** on page 9.

WHAT'S YOUR OPINION?

In the past many wild animals were used in circus shows. Turn to page 17 to read why one girl is happy that some circuses no longer practise this.

PROFILE

Guy Laliberté was once a street kid. Learn on page 22 how he turned his life around and brought the world a whole new kind of circus.

MY DIARY

Pack your bags—you're off to circus camp! Join in the fun on pages 27 and 29 to learn what it's like to ride a unicycle and clown around.

SITESEEING · ART & ENTERTAINMENT

Where were marionettes invented?
Visit **www.infosteps.co.uk**
for more about PUPPETS.

Stilt Walkers

Long ago in the misty marshes of a French village called Les Landes shepherds perched high on wooden stilts to watch over their sheep. In the town women walked to market on stilts and children stomped to school, did their chores and even played games above the soggy ground, all on stilts. Stilt walking was a perfect way of keeping their feet dry.

Stilt walking is a tradition in parts of China where rivers once flooded the streets. During Chinese New Year celebrations today stilt dancers parade through the streets.

Stilt walkers of Les Landes

Stilt walking has been a part of daily living, festival fun and larger-than-life legend in Les Landes and in many places around the world for thousands of years. Tricks with tall sticks have often been passed from generation to generation, and to this day dancers on stilts and long-legged clowns provide fun for everyone.

Mocko Jumbie is a form of stilt walking that began in Ghana, West Africa long ago. Over time the stilt walking became stilt dancing, and today people still watch Mocko Jumbie stilt dancers perform.

Around the World on Stilts

In 1891 a baker from Les Landes strode over mountains and through country after country in a record-setting stilt marathon!

In California farmers use stilts to harvest orchards. As the saying goes, "One pair of stilts is worth a dozen ladders".

In Mexico there are carvings of stilt dancers in ancient ruins. People believed stilt dancers would bring good luck. Some Mexican dancers still perform stilt dances today.

In Sudan a wise man carved short walking sticks so that he could plant seeds without burning his feet on the hot ground. People there still use stilts today.

Stilt Walkers continued

In Europe, during battles of the past, soldiers on stilts crossed moats to invade castles.

In China the Liao River often flooded its banks. The people walked along the streets high and dry on stilts. The river has now changed its course, but stilt walking remains a tradition.

In India people dance on stilts during the spring planting of crops in hope that the crops will grow as tall as the stilt walkers.

In Japan children walk through the first winter snow on bamboo stilts. They also play games on their stilt "bamboo horses".

In Tanzania a stilt dancer named "the man in the tree top" asked for the young people to grow tall and strong and reach their highest dreams.

In New Zealand the Maori have a tale to explain how people lose things. They say tiptoe thieves on stilts snatch things and disappear without leaving a footprint.

Giant Strides

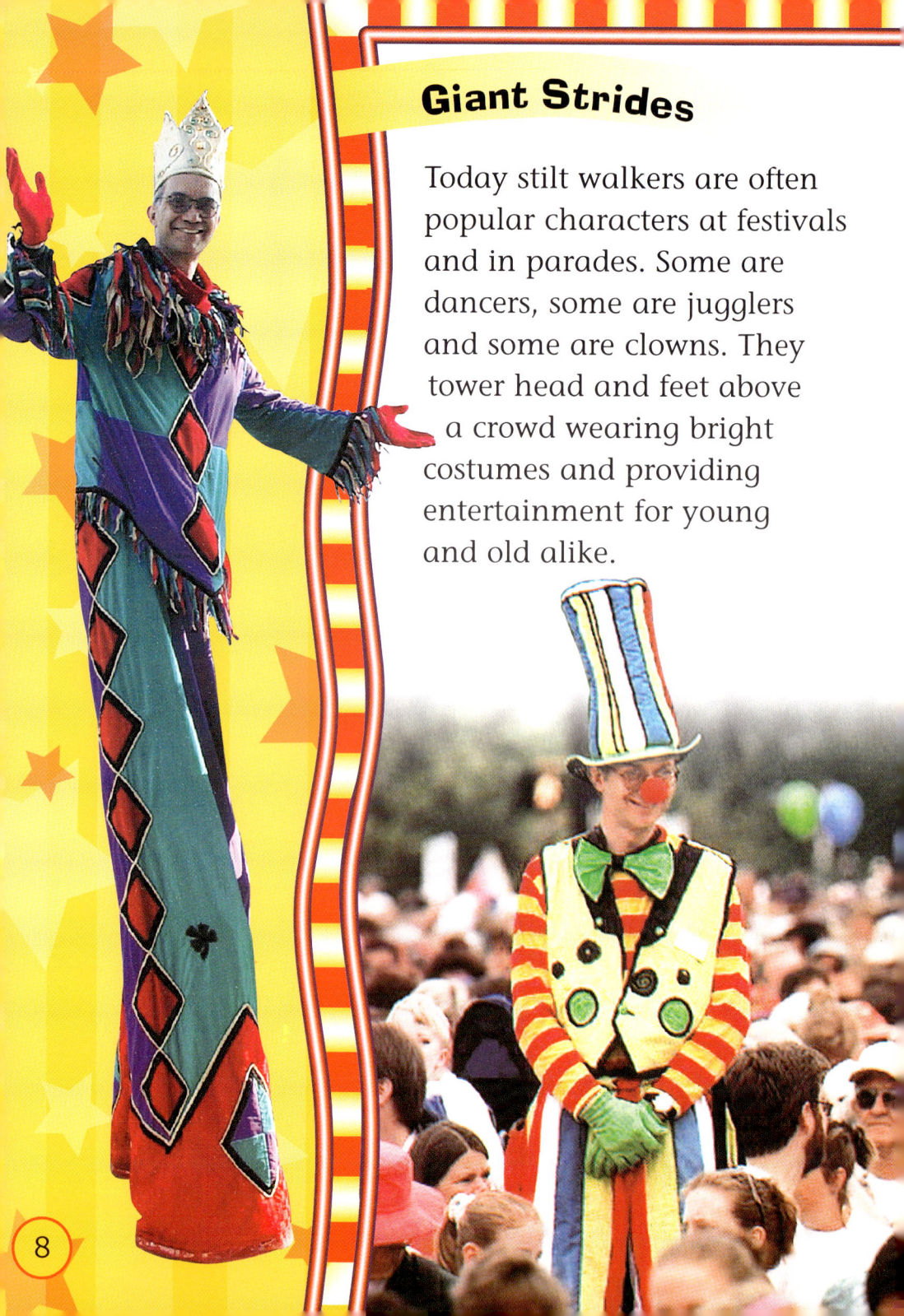

Today stilt walkers are often popular characters at festivals and in parades. Some are dancers, some are jugglers and some are clowns. They tower head and feet above a crowd wearing bright costumes and providing entertainment for young and old alike.

Stilt Walkers continued

Tall Talk

Bill Coleman is a three-metre-tall stilt performer and clown. He began stilt walking at the age of 43. People call him Stretch when they talk up to him.

Q Hi there Stretch! What made you start stilt walking?

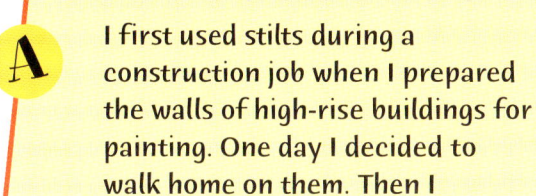

A I first used stilts during a construction job when I prepared the walls of high-rise buildings for painting. One day I decided to walk home on them. Then I thought parades would be fun.

Q Have you ever fallen off your stilts during a parade?

A Yes, but it doesn't happen too often anymore. Once in a big crowd I was knocked over because people didn't see me above them.

Q How long did it take you to feel really steady on stilts?

A It was three months before I could wobble along for several kilometres on my stilts. Parades involve a lot of walking. To get fit I strode along flat ground and stomped up and down hills on my stilts. When I was in training for a marathon I stilt walked for as many as nineteen kilometres at a time.

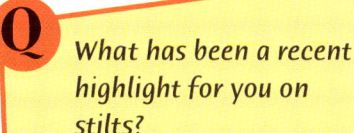

Q What has been a recent highlight for you on stilts?

A I completed a marathon in Dublin, Ireland, on stilts as a fundraiser for a charity. It was sometimes hard to see around the leafy trees so I lost my way now and then. I finished the marathon in less than nine hours, though, and knew my efforts would help people. That was a really good feeling!

Every Street's a Stage

For many performers entertaining a crowd is far more than a job—it's a way of life. While some perform in local parades and at festivals others turn themselves into a travelling road show, providing instant entertainment wherever they go. Talented street performers can often sing, dance, tell stories, juggle and even do **acrobatics**.

Some travelling entertainers today live in colourful mobile homes called house trucks. They travel from town to town.

Travelling entertainers have performed for audiences since medieval times. In Europe **minstrels** and small groups of actors often travelled from village to village performing plays, using a street or marketplace as a stage. Their wagons were loaded with costumes, **props** and make-up as well as everyday items.

This painting by a famous artist named Pieter Brueghel the Younger shows a village festival taking place 400 years ago. A group of travelling actors has set up a temporary stage in the marketplace.

Festival Fun

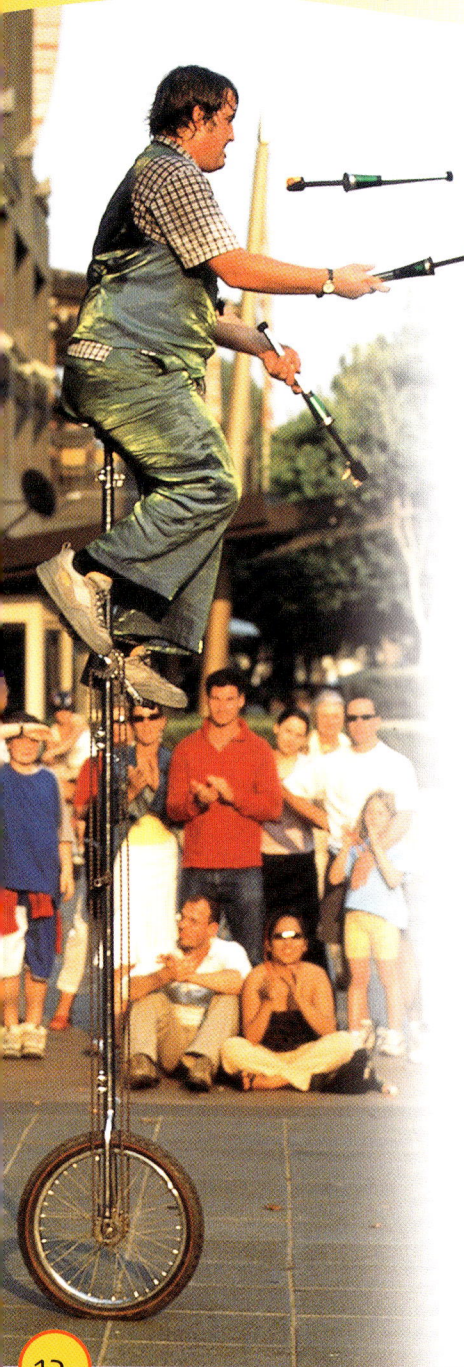

Street performers are known in some places as buskers. These performers may be jugglers, magicians, musicians, **comedians,** actors or mime artists. No two of their performances are the same. People in the audience are often woven into a show and the setting is always new. Street performers will often **improvise,** changing their routine to suit the scene.

No matter what skills they possess talented street performers have one thing in common—they can attract a crowd in the blink of an eye! In fact their acts have become so popular that some cities now have street performance festivals. These annual events are attended by performers from all over the world.

Every Street's a Stage continued

Although street performers sometimes perform without pay they usually pass around a hat at the end of a show so an audience can **tip** them.

Living statues entertain crowds for hours by not moving a muscle!

Puppet Power

In some travelling shows people step behind the scenes and let puppets be the stars. **Puppeteers** control puppets by hand or by strings, wires or rods. Characters in a puppet show might be people or animals. They dance around and get into all sorts of trouble. The audience is often encouraged to join in and shout back at the characters in a puppet show. Their replies can be an important part of the act.

Punch and Judy wrestle with Crocodile.

Every Street's a Stage continued

> Punch and Judy are simple hand, or glove, puppets. Their silly actions and rough-and-tumble **slapstick** comedy have entertained generations of children.

Punch and Judy are characters in a famous puppet show from Europe. Travelling puppeteers have taken the show to festivals and street fairs across England since the 1600s.

Where were marionettes invented?
Visit **www.infosteps.co.uk**
for more about PUPPETS.

Under the Big Top

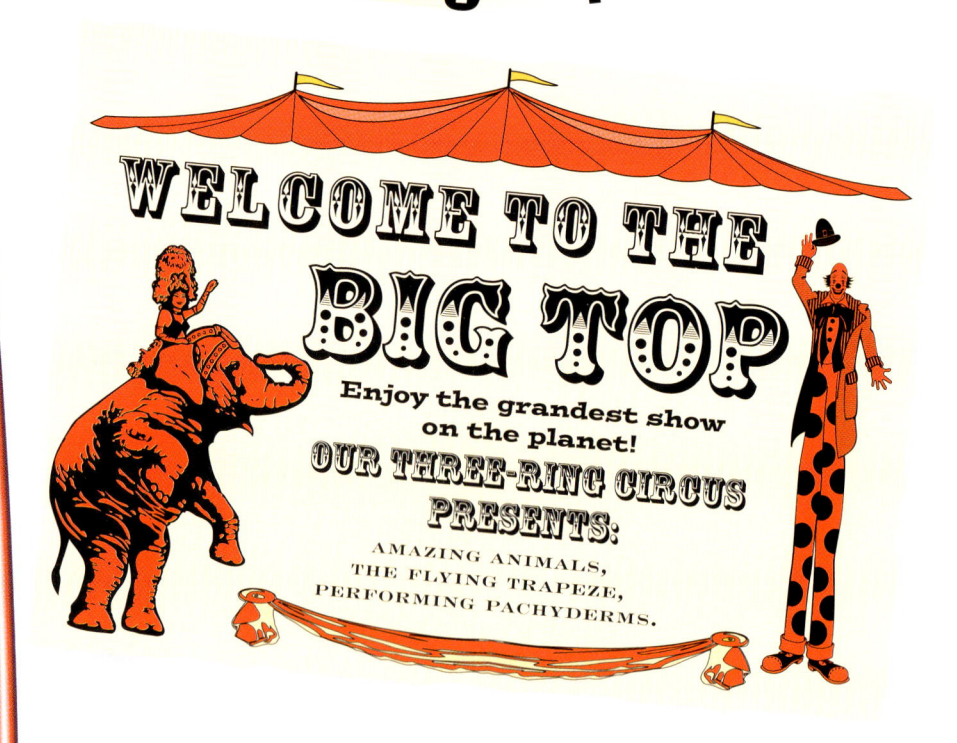

When it comes to travelling shows many people think that a circus is hard to beat. There is always great excitement when a circus comes to town. Brightly lit tents, tempting stalls and performers of every shape and size appear overnight.

Circuses began in Europe hundreds of years ago. During the 1800s the "big top" travelling circus with its canvas tent, its wild animal shows and its colourful clowns and trapeze artists became the most popular form of entertainment in North America.

In the first circuses daring riders rode horses bareback, performing tricks and acrobatics. The idea of a travelling circus with animal shows began in North America. An entire circus "city" could go up in about fourteen hours.

WHAT'S YOUR OPINION?

I think it is a very good thing that some circuses today do not have wild animals such as elephants, tigers and giraffes in their shows. I believe that these beautiful animals should be wild and free in their own natural homes and not trained to perform for humans. What do you think?

Circus with a Difference

Circuses have changed in many ways over the years. Some have developed special community programmes. In the United States *Circus of the Senses*® is a special production designed for children who have difficulty seeing or hearing. It allows these children to experience the wonder and excitement of a circus. Performances feature explanations of the action in the ring and Braille programmes to use during the show. American Sign Language experts interpret the action. After a show some children are invited into the ring for a "touch session" where they join the **cast** for a hands-on experience with animals and props.

IN FOCUS

Clown Doctors

One American circus runs a Clown Care Unit®. Professional performers are specially chosen to be "clown doctors". They are trained to work in hospital settings. They bring laughter and joy to children in hospitals around the country. Through fun and smiles they help children understand operations by performing their own clown medicine, such as "red-nose transplants" and "chocolate-milk transfusions".

Cirque du Soleil

A new kind of circus began in Canada in 1984. This was a circus that focused on the skill and beauty of the human body in motion instead of on animals. Cirque du Soleil was started by a **troupe** of creative young street performers who were not afraid to dream and who were brave enough to risk trying something bold and new. Through their imagination, talent and sheer hard work, they created shows that turned the human body into an instrument of art.

Today more than 2,100 people from forty different nations and twenty-five different language groups work for Cirque du Soleil.

Most Cirque performers are younger than the age of thirty. For the children who perform in Cirque du Soleil lessons are an important part of everyday life. School comes along with every production. On-site classrooms are in trailers, and children study from 11 A.M. until 4 P.M. After that it's show time!

21

PROFILE

Guy Laliberté is now the head of Cirque du Soleil, but his journey began on the streets of Montreal. "I was a street kid," says Guy. "But one day I saw a show in Montreal and I caught fire. I knew right away that entertaining people was what I wanted to do and I believed I could do it. It turned my life around." Guy joined a group of young street performers. They later formed Cirque du Soleil.

Guy has never forgotten his street performer origins. He recently founded a special programme called Cirque du Monde. It helps troubled young people around the world. Performers train youth in circus arts such as juggling and acrobatics. Together they put on shows. Some young people stay with Cirque du Monde to lead programmes for others.

Cirque du Soleil **continued**

All Cirque performers train hard. They practise, practise, practise and perform. Many train in a special studio with high-tech equipment for acrobatics and special effects. Here trampolinists reach for the sky and trapeze artists swing and spin through the air, performing amazing acrobatics. A pit filled with thousands of soft foam cubes cushions any falls.

And why is there all this effort? As one Cirque du Monde volunteer says, "The world needs artists, because artists wake up your sense of wonder—the wonder of being human, of being alive together."

Flying Fruit Flies

Half a world away on the sun-baked continent of Australia, another spectacular circus turns traditional ideas of circus fun completely upside down. Founded in 1979 during the International Year of the Child, the Flying Fruit Fly Circus is designed to capture the imaginations and talents of children across the land.

In this high-energy circus theatre show Flying Fruit Flies turn a school yard into an imaginary big top circus.

Kids who dream of becoming a Fruit Fly performer learn skills such as trampolining, rope climbing, tumbling, juggling and flying through the air on a trapeze. Set to lively music, performances blend circus, dance and theatre. Each year the Flying Fruit Flies amaze audiences in shows around the world.

Australia is a vast land and many communities are located in remote rural areas. Special Flying Fruit Fly projects bring training and entertainment to people in distant towns.

Circus Camp

If circus school doesn't come to you, you might go to circus camp! Many circuses run camps and workshops where professional performers teach youth circus skills such as stilt walking, unicycle riding, tumbling, balancing on a high wire and even how to safely fall on purpose! Students practise and practise so that by the end of camp they are ready to put up ropes and nets, put on costumes and make-up and step into the spotlight for show time!

Ride a unicycle!

July 23

Dear Mum and Dad,

I am having a ball at circus camp! I have only been here for three days, but I've already learned how to juggle, how to balance and even how to ride a unicycle!

It's hard work, though. We practise a lot. We train to get fit too. I have made some really cool friends. See you soon!

From your circus star daughter,
Grace

MR AND MRS COOPER
10 KILLARNEY RD
GLENDENE BAY 1013

Clowning Around

Some people like to make others laugh. Clowns are expert comedians. They often have a box full of tricks and a head full of jokes. Many are talented acrobats. They know how to juggle and how to balance and they often perform a series of funny skits, called gags, where everything seems to go wrong.

Most clowns wear thick brightly coloured make-up, or greasepaint, for a show. A clown works hard to create his or her one-of-a-kind clown face. A clown's face and costume are an important part of the clown's character.

Learn to juggle!

Circus Camp continued

Dear Grandma and Grandpa,

You always said I could be a clown! Well here I am with my very own clown costume. I decided to be a funny clown. I have a funny clown walk and a funny clown wig. I am getting good at putting on funny clown make-up too! I can't wait until you come to see the show we are putting on at the end of camp.

From your clowning around grandson,
Jack

Glossary

acrobatics – spectacular and skillful performances using moves common in gymnastics

cast – the name given to all the actors in an entertainment production

comedian – a person who entertains others by being funny

improvise – to make up something on the spot

minstrel – a travelling entertainer long ago who could sing, dance, play musical instruments, tell stories and act. Minstrels often dressed in colourful costumes so that people would notice them when they came to town.

prop – something that supports another thing. A prop in a play could be an object that helps identify a character, such as a broom for a cleaner.

puppeteer – a person who controls puppets. Puppeteers often remain hidden behind the stage so that it looks as if the puppets are moving on their own.

slapstick – silly comedy full of rough-and-tumble jokes

tip – a gift of money given in thanks for a service

troupe – a group of actors

Index

American Sign Language	18
Braille	18
Brueghel, Pieter	11
Chinese New Year	4
Circus of the Senses®	18
Cirque du Monde	22–23
Cirque du Soleil	20–23
clowns	5, 8–9, 16, 19, 28–29
Coleman, Bill	9
festivals	5, 8, 10–12
Flying Fruit Fly Circus, the	24–25
Laliberté, Guy	22
Les Landes, France	4–6
living statues	13
Mocko Jumbie	5
plays	11
Punch and Judy	14–15
puppets	14–15
school	21, 26
street performers	10–13, 20, 22

Research Starters

1 Study the map and pictures on pages 6–7. Choose a scene and country that interests you. Find out more about the customs and festivals that take place there.

2 Glove puppets and string puppets are just two of many kinds of puppets. Research to learn about other kinds of puppets and puppet shows around the world.

3 Do you notice the small ® symbol on pages 18–19? Find out what this means and why it is sometimes important for people to use a symbol like this.

4 Look through the many different kinds of circuses featured in this book. Choose one and design your own spectacular circus poster. Compare your poster to other posters from the past that you research.